The Currency Convergence

Navigating the Global Monetary Landscape

AUTHOR STELLA M DOUD

Contents

Introduction

In the ever-evolving landscape of global finance, the currencies we use shape the very foundation of our economic systems. From the rise of the US dollar as the world's reserve currency to the emergence of cryptocurrencies challenging traditional monetary structures, the journey of money has been a fascinating and tumultuous one. This book delves into the intricate tapestry of the global monetary system, examining the decline of the US dollar since its inception in 1913 and the disruptive advancements in the cryptocurrency market since 2009. Moreover, it offers insights into navigating these changes, staying abreast of developments, and discerning the currencies that hold the potential to shape the future of finance.

1: The Decline of the US Dollar

1.1: Origins and Ascendancy The establishment of the Federal Reserve System in 1913 marked a pivotal moment in American financial history. Designed to provide stability to the financial system, the Federal Reserve became the guardian of monetary policy, regulating the supply of money and credit in the economy. With the US dollar as its primary instrument, the Federal Reserve wielded significant influence over domestic and global economic affairs.

Following World War II, the Bretton Woods Agreement of 1944 solidified the dominance of the US dollar as the world's reserve currency. Under this agreement, major currencies were pegged to the dollar, which, in turn, was redeemable for gold at a fixed rate of $35 per ounce. This system facilitated international trade and investment, establishing the dollar as the linchpin of the post-war economic order.

Understanding the historical trajectory and contemporary challenges facing the US dollar provides crucial insights into the evolving dynamics of the global monetary system. As we navigate these shifting sands, it is imperative to remain vigilant and adaptable to emerging paradigms of finance and governance.

1.2 Erosion of Dollar Dominance

The 1970s witnessed a series of challenges to the dollar's supremacy, culminating in President Richard Nixon's decision to abandon the gold standard in 1971. Facing mounting trade deficits and inflationary pressures, Nixon unilaterally suspended the dollar's convertibility to gold, effectively severing the link between the dollar and tangible assets. This marked the beginning of an era of fiat currencies, where the value of money was no longer tied to precious metals but rather determined by government decree.

Subsequent decades saw the erosion of the dollar's purchasing power as the United States grappled with burgeoning debt, widening budget deficits, and trade imbalances. The twin shocks of the oil crises in the 1970s and the stagflation of the 1980s underscored the vulnerabilities of the US economy and its currency. Moreover, the rise of emerging economies such as China and the European Union posed formidable challenges to the dollar's hegemony, with regional currencies gaining prominence as alternatives to the greenback.

1.3 Contemporary Challenges

In the wake of the 2008 financial crisis, the Federal Reserve embarked on unprecedented monetary stimulus measures, including quantitative easing and near-zero interest rates, to revive a flagging economy. While these interventions succeeded in averting a systemic collapse, they also raised concerns about the long-term sustainability of the dollar and its status as a safe haven asset.

Furthermore, geopolitical tensions and the weaponization of the dollar as a tool of economic coercion have strained relations between the United States and its trading partners. The extraterritorial reach of US sanctions and the dominance of the dollar in global financial transactions have prompted calls for alternative reserve currencies and payment mechanisms.

As the world grapples with the uncertainties of a multipolar monetary order, the future of the US dollar hangs in the balance. Whether it will retain its preeminence or yield to the forces of economic realignment remains a subject of intense debate and speculation.

2: The Rise of Cryptocurrencies

2.1 Genesis of Bitcoin

The genesis of Bitcoin, with the publication of Satoshi Nakamoto's whitepaper titled "Bitcoin: A Peer-to-Peer Electronic Cash System" in 2008, marked the beginning of a revolutionary new era in finance. Satoshi's vision was to create a decentralized digital currency that operated on a peer-to-peer network, bypassing the need for intermediaries such as banks or financial institutions. Bitcoin, the first cryptocurrency, introduced the concept of blockchain technology—a distributed ledger that records all transactions in a secure and immutable manner.

The decentralized nature of Bitcoin, coupled with its fixed supply and deflationary model, appealed to early adopters and enthusiasts seeking alternatives to traditional fiat currencies. The pseudonymous identity of Satoshi Nakamoto added to the mystique surrounding Bitcoin's origins, fueling intrigue and speculation within online communities.

2.2 Evolution and Expansion

Following the launch of Bitcoin in 2009, a proliferation of alternative cryptocurrencies, or altcoins, emerged, each seeking to address perceived shortcomings or innovate upon Satoshi's original design. Litecoin, launched in 2011, introduced faster transaction times and a different hashing algorithm, while Ripple (XRP) aimed to facilitate cross-border payments and remittances for financial institutions.

The expansion of the cryptocurrency ecosystem gave rise to diverse blockchain applications beyond currency, including smart contracts, decentralized autonomous organizations (DAOs), and tokenized assets. Ethereum, launched in 2015 by Vitalik Buterin, introduced the concept of smart contracts—self-executing agreements coded on the blockchain— which paved the way for decentralized finance (DeFi) platforms and decentralized exchanges (DEXs).

As the cryptocurrency market matured, regulatory scrutiny intensified, with governments and financial regulators grappling with the challenges of classification, taxation, and consumer protection. The proliferation of initial coin offerings (ICOs) and token sales raised concerns about fraud, investor risk, and market manipulation, prompting authorities to impose stricter oversight and enforcement measures.

2.3 Shifting Paradigms

The growing institutional interest in cryptocurrencies and digital assets heralded a new era of mainstream adoption and acceptance. Wall Street titans, including investment banks, hedge funds, and asset managers, began exploring avenues for exposure to Bitcoin and other cryptocurrencies as alternative investments and portfolio diversifiers.

Simultaneously, environmental concerns surrounding the energy consumption and carbon footprint of proof-of-work (PoW) cryptocurrencies like Bitcoin sparked debates about sustainability and scalability. Ethereum's transition to a proof-of-stake (PoS) consensus mechanism and the development of layer 2 scaling solutions aimed to address these challenges while enhancing network efficiency and throughput.

Central banks and governments also entered the fray, exploring the feasibility of central bank digital currencies (CBDCs) as a means to modernize payment systems, enhance financial inclusion, and combat illicit activities. Projects such as China's digital yuan and the European Union's digital euro underscored the growing recognition of blockchain technology as a catalyst for innovation and reform within the traditional banking sector. The rise of cryptocurrencies represents a paradigm shift in the way we conceive of money, value, and trust in the digital age. As blockchain technology continues to evolve and mature, its transformative potential extends far beyond financial transactions, encompassing areas such as supply chain management, identity verification, and decentralized governance. By understanding the origins, evolution, and implications of cryptocurrencies, we can better navigate the complexities of the digital economy and harness its benefits for the collective good.

3: Navigating the Monetary Maze

3.1 Staying Informed

In today's fast-paced financial landscape, staying informed is paramount to making informed decisions about investments and monetary matters. Utilizing reputable sources such as financial news websites, industry publications, and regulatory announcements can provide valuable insights into macroeconomic trends, policy developments, and market sentiment.

Understanding the broader economic context and geopolitical dynamics that influence currency movements and asset prices is essential for navigating the volatile terrain of global finance. Engaging with online communities, forums, and social media platforms allows individuals to exchange ideas, share perspectives, and stay abreast of emerging trends and opportunities.
Moreover, attending conferences, webinars, and seminars hosted by industry experts and thought leaders provides opportunities for networking, learning, and professional development. By cultivating a diverse array of informational resources and maintaining a curious, inquisitive mindset, individuals can enhance their financial literacy and decision-making prowess in an ever-changing world.

3.2 Assessing Cryptocurrency Projects

Evaluating cryptocurrency projects requires a comprehensive understanding of technical, economic, and regulatory factors that impact their viability and potential for long-term success. Conducting due diligence on project fundamentals, team credentials, and development roadmap is crucial for mitigating risks and identifying promising investment opportunities. Assessing technological innovation, scalability, and security features of blockchain platforms and protocols can provide insights into their ability to address real-world problems and gain traction in competitive markets. Analyzing community engagement, social media presence, and sentiment indicators can offer valuable clues about market dynamics and investor sentiment.

Furthermore, considering regulatory compliance, legal risks, and geopolitical considerations is essential for navigating the complex regulatory landscape and mitigating legal liabilities. Engaging with legal experts, regulatory consultants, and compliance professionals can provide guidance and assurance in navigating legal and regulatory challenges.

3.3 Diversification and Risk Management

Diversification and risk management are fundamental **principles of** prudent investing and wealth preservation in any financial market. Building a diversified portfolio across asset classes, geographies, and sectors can help mitigate concentration risk and enhance portfolio resilience against market volatility and unforeseen events.

Implementing risk management strategies such as dollar-cost averaging, asset allocation, and rebalancing allows investors to maintain discipline and stay focused on long-term financial goals amid short-term fluctuations and market uncertainties. Setting realistic investment objectives, time horizons, and risk tolerance levels is essential for aligning investment strategies with individual preferences and circumstances Remaining vigilant against scams, phishing attempts, and security breaches in the cryptocurrency space requires adopting robust cybersecurity practices and exercising caution when interacting with digital assets and online platforms. Utilizing hardware wallets, multi-factor authentication, and encryption technologies can help safeguard personal and financial information from unauthorized access and malicious attacks.

By adopting a disciplined, diversified approach to investing and risk management, individuals can navigate the complexities of the global monetary system with confidence and resilience, positioning themselves for long-term financial success and prosperity.

Navigating the monetary maze requires a blend of knowledge, prudence, and adaptability in responding to evolving market dynamics and emerging opportunities. By equipping themselves with the tools, insights, and strategies outlined in this chapter, individuals can navigate the complexities of the global monetary landscape with confidence and resilience, positioning themselves for financial success and security in an increasingly interconnected world.

In the dynamic world of cryptocurrency markets, understanding key terms is crucial for evaluating investment opportunities and estimating future valuations of coins and tokens. Here, we explore essential terms and their significance:

3.4a: Market Capitalization (Market Cap):

Market capitalization refers to the total value of a cryptocurrency in circulation and is calculated by multiplying the current price per coin or token by the total supply.

Significance: Market cap provides insights into the relative size and dominance of a cryptocurrency within the broader market. It helps investors gauge the potential growth and stability of a cryptocurrency and compare it to others in the market.

3.4 b: Circulating Supply:

Circulating supply refers to the total number of coins or tokens that are actively traded and available in the market.

Significance: Understanding circulating supply is essential for assessing a cryptocurrency's liquidity, scarcity, and potential price appreciation. Coins with limited circulating supply may exhibit greater price volatility and potential for rapid price movements.

3.4c: Total Supply:

Total supply represents the maximum number of coins or tokens that will ever be created or mined for a cryptocurrency.

Significance: Total supply influences inflation rates, scarcity, and long-term sustainability of a cryptocurrency. Cryptocurrencies with capped or deflationary supplies may be perceived as more valuable and resistant to inflationary pressures.

3.4d: Volume (Trading Volume):

Volume refers to the total number of coins or tokens traded within a specific time period, typically measured in terms of currency (e.g., USD).

Significance: Volume indicates the level of market activity, liquidity, and investor interest in a cryptocurrency. Higher trading volumes often signify greater market participation and confidence in the asset.

3.4e: Price Volatility:

Price volatility measures the degree of fluctuation in a cryptocurrency's price over time.

Significance: Understanding price volatility is crucial for assessing risk and potential returns in cryptocurrency investments. High volatility can present opportunities for profit but also increases the risk of significant losses.

3.4f: Liquidity:

Liquidity refers to the ease with which a cryptocurrency can be bought or sold in the market without causing significant price slippage.

Significance: Liquidity is essential for executing trades efficiently and minimizing transaction costs. Cryptocurrencies with higher liquidity are generally preferred by traders and investors due to their ability to enter and exit positions without impacting market prices.

3.4g: Market Sentiment:

Market sentiment reflects the overall mood and perception of investors

towards a particular cryptocurrency or the market as a whole.
Significance: Market sentiment influences price movements, trading activity, and investment decisions. Positive sentiment may drive buying pressure and price appreciation, while negative sentiment can lead to selling pressure and price depreciation.
Understanding these key cryptocurrency market terms empowers investors to make informed decisions, assess risks, and identify opportunities for growth and wealth creation in the dynamic and rapidly evolving world of digital assets.

4: Charting the Future of Finance

4.1 Interoperability and Integration

Interoperability refers to the ability of disparate blockchain networks and digital assets to seamlessly communicate, transact, and exchange value with one another. As the cryptocurrency ecosystem continues to expand, interoperability protocols and cross-chain solutions are emerging to bridge the divide between siloed blockchain platforms and foster greater connectivity and collaboration.

Projects such as Polkadot, Cosmos, and Avalanche are pioneering interoperability solutions that enable interoperability between diverse blockchain networks, facilitating the transfer of assets and data across multiple chains. These interoperability protocols aim to unlock new synergies, efficiencies, and opportunities for innovation by breaking down barriers to entry and enabling seamless interoperability between blockchain ecosystems.

The vision of a universal ledger that unifies global currencies and assets holds the promise of greater efficiency, transparency, and inclusivity in the global financial system. By fostering interoperability and integration, blockchain technology has the potential to democratize finance, empower individuals, and catalyze the emergence of a truly borderless, decentralized economy.

4.2 Democratizing Finance

The democratization of finance represents a paradigm shift in the way financial services are accessed, delivered, and consumed in the digital age. Blockchain technology and decentralized finance (DeFi) platforms are leveling the playing field, empowering individuals with unprecedented access to financial services, investment opportunities, and wealth-building tools.

DeFi platforms such as Uniswap, Compound, and Aave enable users to borrow, lend, trade, and earn interest on digital assets without the need for traditional intermediaries such as banks or brokerage firms. By leveraging smart contracts and decentralized protocols, DeFi platforms facilitate peer-to-peer transactions, automated lending, and algorithmic trading, reducing friction, costs, and inefficiencies associated with traditional finance.

The rise of decentralized autonomous organizations (DAOs) and community-driven governance models is reshaping the landscape of corporate governance, decision-making, and value creation. DAOs enable participants to collectively govern, fund, and govern projects and initiatives in a transparent, decentralized manner, fostering collaboration, accountability, and alignment of incentives.

By democratizing access to financial services, investment opportunities, and governance mechanisms, blockchain technology is democratizing finance, empowering individuals, and communities to participate in the global economy on their own terms.

4.3 Embracing the Unknown

The future of finance is characterized by uncertainty, complexity, and rapid change, as technological innovation, regulatory evolution, and geopolitical dynamics continue to reshape the global monetary landscape. Embracing the unknown requires a mindset of curiosity, adaptability, and resilience in the face of uncertainty and disruption. Technological advancements such as artificial intelligence, machine learning, and quantum computing are poised to transform the way financial services are delivered, consumed, and regulated, unlocking new capabilities, efficiencies, and opportunities for innovation.

Regulatory frameworks and policy initiatives play a crucial role in shaping the trajectory of the cryptocurrency market, influencing market dynamics, investor sentiment, and adoption trends. As governments and regulators grapple with the challenges and opportunities posed by blockchain technology, collaboration, dialogue, and experimentation are essential for fostering an enabling regulatory environment that promotes innovation while safeguarding consumer protection and market integrity.

Embracing the unknown requires a willingness to experiment, iterate, and learn from both successes and failures, as we collectively navigate the uncharted waters of the digital economy. By embracing uncertainty as an opportunity for growth, exploration, and discovery, we can unlock the full potential of blockchain technology to transform finance, empower individuals, and create a more equitable, , and sustainable future for all.

Charting the future of finance requires a collective effort to harness the transformative potential of blockchain technology, decentralized finance, and digital assets to create a more inclusive, resilient, and equitable global financial system. By fostering interoperability, democratizing access to financial services, and embracing uncertainty as an opportunity for innovation and growth, we can chart a course towards a brighter, more prosperous future for generations to come.

5: New Scientific Discoveries

5.1 Unraveling the Mysteries of the Universe
Breakthroughs in particle physics, cosmology,
 and quantum mechanics have revolutionized our understanding of the universe and our place within it. From discovering the Higgs boson at CERN's Large Hadron Collider to detecting gravitational waves from merging black holes and neutron stars, scientists continue to push the boundaries of knowledge and exploration.
The quest to understand dark matter and dark energy, comprising over 95% of the universe's total mass-energy content, remains one of the most compelling mysteries in modern physics. Observations of the cosmic microwave background radiation, galactic rotation curves, and large-scale structure formation provide clues to the nature of dark matter and its gravitational effects on the cosmos.
Advancements in quantum computing, quantum entanglement, and quantum teleportation offer insights into the fundamental principles governing the behavior of matter and energy at the smallest scales. The development of quantum algorithms and quantum sensors holds promise for applications in cryptography, materials science, and precision measurement.
The convergence of theoretical physics, experimental cosmology, and computational modeling is reshaping our understanding of reality, challenging conventional wisdom, and inspiring new generations of scientists and explorers to unravel the mysteries of the universe.
5.2 Genomics and Biotechnology
Advances in genomics, gene editing, and biotechnology are transforming healthcare, agriculture, and environmental sustainability. The advent of next-generation sequencing technologies has enabled scientists to decode the human genome, identify disease-causing mutations, and develop targeted therapies for cancer, genetic disorders, and infectious diseases.

CRISPR-Cas9, a revolutionary gene-editing tool, allows researchers to precisely modify DNA sequences, correct genetic defects, and engineer novel traits in plants, animals, and microorganisms. The potential applications of CRISPR range from curing genetic diseases and enhancing crop yields to combating antibiotic resistance and mitigating climate change. The emergence of synthetic biology, biomimicry, and regenerative medicine is blurring the boundaries between living and non-living systems, offering new avenues for innovation, discovery, and collaboration across disciplines. From bio-inspired materials and biofuels to tissue engineering and organ transplantation, biotechnology is reshaping the landscape of human health and well-being.

Ethical considerations, regulatory oversight, and societal implications surrounding genetic engineering and biotechnological interventions raise profound questions about human nature, identity, and the future of life on Earth. As scientists and policymakers navigate the ethical and moral complexities of biotechnology, the pursuit of knowledge and the quest for human betterment remain guiding principles in the exploration of the frontiers of life and consciousness.

By exploring the frontiers of genomics, biotechnology, and the mysteries of the universe, scientists and researchers are pushing the boundaries of human knowledge and discovery. As we continue to unlock the secrets of nature and harness the power of technology for the benefit of humanity, the journey towards a more sustainable, equitable, and enlightened future unfolds before us, inviting us to explore, innovate, and aspire to greater heights of understanding and wonder.

6: Space Exploration

6.1 The New Space Race

The 21st century has witnessed a resurgence of interest in space exploration, fueled by technological advancements, entrepreneurial vision, and international collaboration. The New Space Race is characterized by the rise of private space companies, government agencies, and international partnerships striving to push the boundaries of human exploration and discovery beyond Earth's atmosphere.

Commercialization of space exploration has democratized access to space, opening up opportunities for scientific research, satellite deployment, and human spaceflight. Companies like SpaceX, Blue Origin, and Virgin Galactic are pioneering reusable rocket technology, reducing the cost and complexity of launching payloads and passengers into orbit.

Lunar exploration has emerged as a focal point of renewed interest, with plans for crewed missions to establish sustainable habitats, resource extraction facilities, and scientific outposts on the Moon's surface. The Artemis program, led by NASA, aims to return humans to the Moon by 2024, laying the groundwork for future missions to Mars and beyond.

The search for extraterrestrial life, whether microbial or intelligent, remains a driving force behind space exploration, as scientists explore the habitability of distant exoplanets, moons, and celestial bodies within our solar system and beyond. Breakthroughs in astrobiology, planetary science, and astrochemistry offer tantalizing clues to the origins of life and the prevalence of habitable environments in the cosmos.

6.2 Satellite Technology and Beyond

Satellite technology has revolutionized communication, navigation,

Earth observation, and scientific research, facilitating global connectivity, disaster response, and environmental monitoring. The proliferation of small satellites and constellations, powered by advances in miniaturization, propulsion, and launch capabilities, is revolutionizing the space industry and enabling new applications and services.

Satellite constellations like SpaceX's Starlink, OneWeb, and Amazon's Project Kuiper promise to provide high-speed internet access to underserved regions, remote communities, and maritime vessels around the world. These mega-constellations, comprised of thousands of interconnected satellites in low Earth orbit (LEO), have the potential to bridge the digital divide, empower education, and spur economic development in remote and marginalized areas.

Applications of satellite technology extend beyond telecommunications to Earth observation, climate monitoring, disaster management, and environmental sustainability. High-resolution imaging satellites, synthetic aperture radar (SAR) systems, and hyperspectral sensors enable scientists to monitor deforestation, track wildlife migration patterns, and assess the impact of climate change on ecosystems and biodiversity.

The future of satellite technology holds promise for breakthroughs in space-based internet, space tourism, space manufacturing, and space debris mitigation. As we venture further into space and unlock the full potential of satellite technology, the possibilities for innovation, exploration, and discovery are limited only by our imagination and ingenuity.

Space exploration represents humanity's quest to explore, understand, **and transcend the limits of our world and venture into the cosmos. As we embark on this epic journey of discovery and adventure, we are reminded of our shared humanity, interconnectedness, and collective destiny as stewards of Earth and explorers of the universe.**

7: Technological Advancements

Artificial intelligence (AI) and machine learning (ML) represent the frontier of computing, enabling machines to learn from data, adapt to new information, and perform tasks traditionally requiring human intelligence. The rapid advancement of AI and ML algorithms has transformed industries ranging from healthcare and finance to transportation and entertainment.

In healthcare, AI-powered diagnostic tools, predictive analytics, and personalized treatment recommendations are revolutionizing patient care, disease detection, and drug discovery. Machine learning algorithms can analyze medical images, genetic data, and electronic health records to identify patterns, predict outcomes, and optimize treatment protocols.

In finance, algorithmic trading, robo-advisors, and fraud detection systems leverage AI and ML techniques to analyze market data, detect anomalies, and make real-time investment decisions. Natural language processing (NLP) algorithms can parse news articles, social media feeds, and corporate filings to extract insights, sentiment analysis, and market trends.

In transportation, autonomous vehicles, traffic management systems, and predictive maintenance algorithms rely on AI and ML models to optimize routes, reduce congestion, and enhance safety on roads and highways. Machine learning algorithms can process sensor data, lidar scans, and camera feeds to navigate complex environments, avoid obstacles, and make split-second decisions.

The potential applications of AI and ML are limitless, with implications for education, cybersecurity, energy, and beyond. As we harness the power of artificial intelligence to augment human intelligence, we must remain vigilant about ethical considerations, bias mitigation, and societal impacts to ensure that AI serves humanity's best interests and advances the common good.

7.2 Quantum Computing and Cryptography

Quantum computing represents a paradigm shift in computational science, harnessing the principles of quantum mechanics to perform calculations that are beyond the capabilities of classical computers. Quantum bits, or qubits, can exist in multiple states simultaneously, enabling exponential speedups in solving complex optimization problems, simulating quantum systems, and breaking cryptographic codes.

In cryptography, quantum computers pose a threat to traditional encryption schemes, such as RSA and ECC, which rely on the difficulty of factoring large numbers and solving discrete logarithm problems. Quantum algorithms, such as Shor's algorithm, can factor large integers and compute discrete logarithms exponentially faster than classical algorithms, rendering current encryption standards vulnerable to attacks.

Post-quantum cryptography aims to develop quantum-resistant encryption schemes and cryptographic protocols that can withstand attacks from quantum adversaries. Lattice-based cryptography, hash-based signatures, and code-based cryptography are among the promising candidates for securing communications, data, and transactions in the quantum era.

In quantum computing, researchers are exploring applications in optimization, machine learning, chemistry, and materials science. Quantum annealing, quantum supremacy, and quantum error correction are active areas of research and development, with implications for drug discovery, materials design, and climate modeling.

As quantum computing matures and becomes more accessible, it has the potential to revolutionize industries, accelerate scientific discovery, and unlock new frontiers of innovation. By investing in quantum technology, fostering collaboration, and addressing technical challenges, we can harness the power of quantum computing to solve some of the most pressing problems facing humanity.

The convergence of artificial intelligence, machine learning, and quantum computing represents a new frontier of technological innovation, with profound implications for society, economy, and humanity's collective future. As we navigate the opportunities and challenges of the digital age, we must embrace the transformative potential of these technologies to create a more equitable, sustainable, and prosperous world for generations to come.

8: Seizing Investment Opportunities

8.1 Identifying Promising Companies
Identifying promising companies entails a comprehensive analysis of various factors to gauge their potential for growth and investment opportunities. Fundamental analysis involves examining a company's financial health, including its revenue streams, profit margins, debt levels, and cash flow. Understanding the stability and growth trajectory of these financial metrics can provide valuable insights into a company's overall performance and potential for future success.
Assessing a company's business model, competitive advantages, and market positioning is crucial for evaluating its long-term viability and growth prospects. Analyzing industry trends, customer preferences, and technological advancements can help investors identify companies that are well-positioned to capitalize on emerging opportunities and navigate competitive challenges.
Utilizing quantitative tools, such as financial ratios, valuation multiples, and discounted cash flow (DCF) analysis, can help investors assess the intrinsic value of a company's stock and determine whether it is undervalued or overvalued relative to its peers and the broader market. By conducting thorough research and analysis, investors can identify promising companies with strong fundamentals and growth potential that may offer attractive investment opportunities.
8.2 Evaluating Early-Stage Investments
Evaluating early-stage investments requires a unique set of considerations and due diligence processes due to the higher risk and uncertainty associated with startups and emerging technologies. Assessing the market opportunity and potential demand for a company's products or services is

essential for evaluating its growth potential and scalability. Understanding the competitive landscape, customer needs, and regulatory environment can help investors assess the feasibility and market fit of a startup's business model.

Analyzing the management team's experience, expertise, and track record is critical for evaluating their ability to execute the company's business plan and navigate challenges along the way. Assessing the strength of the team's vision, leadership, and commitment to innovation can provide insights into their ability to drive growth and create value for investors.

Diversifying investment portfolio across multiple early-stage ventures, sectors, and geographies can help mitigate risks and enhance the overall return potential. Engaging with startup accelerators, venture capital firms, and industry networks can provide access to deal flow, due diligence resources, and investment opportunities in promising startups and emerging technologies.

By conducting thorough research, building relationships with entrepreneurs and industry experts, and diversifying investment portfolio, investors can position themselves to capitalize on the growth potential of early-stage ventures while managing risks associated with investing in startups and emerging technologies.

8.3 Staying Ahead of the Curve

Staying ahead of the curve requires a proactive approach to monitoring market trends, technological advancements, and regulatory developments that may impact investment opportunities. Engaging with industry experts, attending conferences, and participating in networking events can provide valuable insights into emerging trends, disruptive technologies, and investment themes.

Remaining informed about macroeconomic indicators, geopolitical risks, and regulatory changes can help investors anticipate market shifts and adjust their investment strategies accordingly. Analyzing industry reports, research publications, and financial news can provide valuable insights into market dynamics, investor sentiment, and emerging opportunities across different sectors and asset classes.

Maintaining a disciplined approach to investment decision-making, including setting clear investment objectives, conducting thorough research, and adhering to risk management principles, is essential for navigating market volatility and uncertainty. By staying focused on long-term investment goals and maintaining a diversified portfolio, investors can weather market fluctuations and capitalize on opportunities for growth and wealth creation.

Embracing innovation, resilience, and adaptability is crucial for navigating the evolving landscape of investment opportunities and positioning oneself for long-term financial success. By staying informed, remaining disciplined, and staying true to one's investment principles, investors can seize opportunities, mitigate risks, and achieve their financial goals in an ever-changing market environment.

By adopting a disciplined approach to investment analysis, risk management, and staying informed about market trends, investors can position themselves to capitalize on opportunities and navigate the complexities of the investment landscape effectively.

Section 2

9: The Paradigm Shift in International Trade and Relations

In the digital era, advances in technology and communications have ushered in profound transformations in the landscape of international trade and relations. This chapter explores the dynamic shifts propelled by technological innovations, emphasizing the transition towards collaboration while also addressing the resistance from individuals and nationalist groups.

9.1 Technological Advancements Driving Collaboration

The advent of technology has dismantled traditional barriers to international trade and fostered unprecedented levels of collaboration among nations. Key advancements, such as the internet, blockchain, and artificial intelligence, have streamlined supply chains, facilitated cross-border transactions, and enhanced communication channels. These innovations have transcended geographical boundaries, enabling real-time interaction and cooperation on a global scale.

9.2 From Competition to Collaboration

In contrast to the zero-sum mentality of the past, contemporary paradigms emphasize collaboration over competition in international trade and relations. Collaborative frameworks, such as multinational trade agreements and economic alliances, have emerged as vehicles for mutual benefit and prosperity. Through collective efforts, nations have sought to leverage comparative advantages, share resources, and address common challenges, fostering a climate of interdependence and cooperation.

9.3 Resistance and Pushback

Despite the transformative potential of technological progress, resistance to change persists among certain individuals and nationalist groups. Fueled by concerns over job displacement, cultural homogenization, and loss of sovereignty, these factions advocate for protectionist policies and isolationist ideologies. Their resistance to globalization and technological integration reflects broader anxieties surrounding identity, security, and economic stability.

9.4 Navigating the Tension

As the forces of collaboration and resistance converge, navigating the tension between technological advancement and socio-political backlash becomes imperative. Policymakers, industry leaders, and civil society must confront the complexities of globalization while safeguarding against its unintended consequences. Balancing the imperatives of innovation with the imperatives of equity and inclusivity requires strategic foresight, adaptive governance, and meaningful dialogue among stakeholders.

9.5 Towards Inclusive Globalization

Ultimately, the trajectory of international trade and relations hinges on the collective ability to embrace inclusive globalization. By harnessing the transformative power of technology while addressing the concerns of marginalized communities and vulnerable populations, societies can forge a path towards sustainable development and shared prosperity. Through dialogue, cooperation, and empathy, nations can transcend narrow interests and forge a future defined by collaboration, resilience, and mutual respect.

In conclusion, the paradigm shift catalyzed by advances in technology and communications presents both opportunities and challenges for international trade and relations. By embracing the principles of collaboration, inclusivity, and adaptability, societies can navigate the complexities of globalization while honoring diverse perspectives and aspirations.